Networking Inside a Company

90 Minute Guides

Michelle N. Halsey

ISBN-10: 1-64004-028-5
ISBN-13: 978-1-64004-028-1

Contents

Chapter 1 – Networking Inside a Company

Networking is unavoidable in modern society. Many people focus on external networking, but the networking process must be used with the company in order to be truly effective. By following the information outlined in this publication, you will be able to network effectively and reap the rewards that come with making connections within the organization.

At the end of this chapter, you should be able to:

- Define networking

- Understand networking principles

- Use networking tools

- Avoid common mistakes

- Understand how to build relationships

- Manage time successfully

The Benefits of Networking at Work

It is easy to overlook the need to make connections within your own organization. The benefits of networking at work, however, are valuable to any career. These benefits include the shared knowledge and increased opportunities. Networking within the organization will also improve your professional image.

Gain Connections

Never underestimate the importance of making connections at work. The personal relationships that you create at work will grow your network in more ways than one. You are directly connected with your coworker, but you are also indirectly connected with the members of your coworker's network. Every connection that you make increases your chances of being referred for new opportunities and greater responsibility.

Shared Knowledge

Networking at work provides the ideal opportunity for shared knowledge. Knowledge sharing is a two-way street. When your connections share knowledge, you will learn how to avoid the mistakes they made and benefit from their experience. Additionally, the information that your connections provide will help inspire new ideas.

Sharing your own knowledge provides its own benefits. When you are able to share valuable information with contacts, you can develop your reputation and expertise. In turn, you can create opportunities for yourself.

Increase Opportunity

Networking in the workplace helps increase opportunity. By having many people in your network, your reputation will quickly spread beyond your immediate peers. As your network develops, word of your skills and expertise will reach superiors and other departments. You will be viewed for your entire skill set rather than by your job description alone. Opportunities that may develop because of your connections include training, mentoring, lateral moves, and promotion.

Improve Image

Creating a network allows you to fine tune your professional image as you connect with others. You can share your successes with your network and conduct yourself in a way that people admire. This provides you with the perfect opportunity to improve your professional image among your peers and superiors. If you take advantage of all the opportunities that networking provides, your professional image will be everything that you want it to be. There are a few tips to improving your image:

- Be helpful

- Be professional

- Share knowledge

Networking Obstacles

Like every endeavor in life, you will face obstacles in your networking. Fortunately, you will be able to navigate and avoid many of these obstacles by correctly defining networking and swallowing your pride. Additionally, the ability to identify difficult personality traits and cultural barriers will provide you with opportunities to avoid miscommunications and facilitate functional relationships

Confusion About The Definition Of Networking

There is some confusion over the definition of networking, which is why many people fail to network effectively. Some people assume that networking is simply meeting new people and collecting their contact information. Others equate networking with socializing. The problem with both definitions is that neither results in true business connections. In true networking, developing contacts and relationships results in new knowledge and greater influence.

By understanding what networking truly is, you will be able to focus your energy appropriately and develop beneficial relationships. We will explore ways to achieve this definition in the following modules.

Personality Traits

Each person has a unique personality. Unfortunately, different personality traits will clash with each other. If you do not know how to handle different personalities, you will encounter obstacles in your networking attempts.

Personality examples:

- Extroverted and playful: These people require more attention and verbal approval than some other personalities.

- Assertive leaders: This type of personality requires loyalty and recognition of achievements.

- Meticulous planners: Meticulous people need the space to complete the tasks, and their perfectionist habits require understanding.

- Peacemakers: Peacemakers work to avoid and settle conflict. They require a calm work environment and appreciation for their efforts.

These are just an overview of personalities. You probably want to research different personalities on your own.

Cultural Barriers

You are likely to encounter cultural barriers in the modern workplace. A diverse work environment provides numerous benefits. A blend of different cultures, however, is likely to result in the miscommunications and conflict. You need to be aware cultural barriers and develop sensitivity towards different people and customs.

Barriers:

- Language: Overcome language barriers with translators and listening carefully. It is also advisable to learn other languages.

- Stereotypes: Monitor your thoughts and feelings to identify any prejudices or stereotypes that would keep you from developing relationships with people from different cultures.

- Cultural Norms: Take the time to understand what normal and respectful behavior is in other cultures. For example, some cultures find making eye contact rude and others do not approve of emotional displays.

Personal Pride

In many instances, personal pride is a benefit. It creates confidence and showcases your talent. In networking, however, personal pride can become a barrier to success. Pride can prevent people from networking effectively. Many people develop relationships but fail to call upon people in their network for help because of their pride. Remember that definition of networking. If you allow your pride to prevent you from using your network, there is no point in having one in the first place.

Chapter 2 – Networking Principles

Now that you know the basic definition of networking and how to avoid common obstacles, it is time to learn the basic networking principles. Networking requires you to build relationships. You need to listen to the people in your network, offer value, and build trust. As you master the basic principles of networking, you will begin to see your network develop.

Relationships

Networking requires building true relationships. Like any other relationship, networking requires time and energy. If you are not willing to put the effort into building new relationships, there is not point in networking. We will delve deeper into relationship building later, but here are some common sense methods to building relationships.

- Communicate with your contacts – Communication is necessary for any relationship.

- Avoid constantly asking for help – While your contacts are resources, being needy is very off-putting.

- Personalize conversation – Get to know your contacts and take interest in their lives.

Listen

It is easy to underestimate the importance of listening when networking. While networking requires selling yourself, it is more than a sales pitch. You need to listen in order to build relationships and network effectively. Do not just allow the other person to talk, actively listening will ensure that you truly understand what the other person is saying.

Tips for Listening:

- Keep eye contact.

- Avoid fidgeting or checking your phone.

- Ask pertinent questions, but do not interrupt

- Pay attention.

- Rephrase what is said.

Offer Value

As we have already stated, networking is a two-way street. You cannot simply expect your contacts to support you and share their knowledge if there is no value in it for them. You must show new contacts that you are an asset. Offering value requires you to understand your networks.

How to Offer Value:

- Identify the needs of others.

- Determine how your expertise meets these needs.

- Offer to help.

Do not over complicate offering value. It can be something as simple as helping a coworker install a new program or sharing notes from a missed meeting.

Build Trust

Trust is needed for every functional relationship, and networking is no different. Your contacts need to feel that you can be trusted. Building trust with new people takes time, but it is not that difficult to accomplish if you pay attention to your behavior.

Steps to Building Trust:

- Be honest – Trust is easier to build when people are honest.

- Act with consistency – Be a mindful employee every day, not just when the boss is around.

- Be helpful – Do not be seen as a self-serving coworker who is willing to do anything to succeed.

Chapter 3 – How to Build Networks

Now that you understand the principles of networking, it is time to address building your network. The guidelines to building networks require using basic common sense. They may seem too simplistic at first glance, but they are essential and must not be overlooked.

Meet New People

Telling you that you need to meet new people to build a network may seem like pointing out the obvious, but this step is often over looked. If you are passive about meeting people, you will never be able to build you network. Meeting people requires action; do not simply wait for people to come to you. Here are a few tips to help you expand your social circle in the workplace:

- Introduce yourself to people – This may be difficult for shy personalities, but it is unlikely that you will be introduced to everyone, particularly in larger organizations, so you must do it yourself.

- Invite people to join you for lunch – This extends to other events.

- Attend groups and functions – These groups and functions may be official or unofficial. Just take the time to meet new people.

Be Polite

It is easy to forget manners in our fast-paced society. Being polite, however, will help you stand out and improve the way that other people view you. It makes you appear more personable and trustworthy. You do not need to be Miss Manners to be polite. Simply exercise common courtesy. Here are a few steps that you can take to being polite.

- Make a good impression: Dress appropriately and address people respectfully at work.

- Pay attention to people: Do not pay attention to your phone or anything else while people are talking to you at work.

- Be considerate: Help other people when you can.

- Think before acting or speaking: Consider the implications of your words or actions, and avoid the workplace dramas.

No matter how hard you try to be polite, you will accidentally offend someone. It is unavoidable. The only way to move past it is to apologize promptly.

Follow up

After meeting new people, it is important to follow up with them. This part of the networking experience can be awkward, so it must be approached carefully. There are different ways you can follow up with people: email, phone, face-to-face, etc. It is possible that you will have to briefly remind your contact of your last encounter, so be prepared to give a few details, Do not, however, spend too much time on this. It is important that you move forward, show the value in your relationship, and prepare the next step. There are different ways to accomplish this early on in the process.

- Suggest an article or book based on the previous meeting.

- Continue your conversation if possible.

- Extend an invitation.

Once you have followed up with your contact, it is up to the other person to respond.

Allow Relationships to Develop Naturally

All relationships have a natural development that should not be rushed. While it is important to follow-up with people, you must avoid appearing desperate or clingy. You will not be able to develop a relationship with everyone, and it is important that you are able to take no for an answer. As a general rule of thumb, you should only contact people three times before they return communication. If they do not contact you, it is best to leave them alone.

Even if your contact has followed up with you, it is important that you do not become an overbearing stalker. This requires common sense. Consider the frequency that you would be comfortable with new people contacting you. Allow this to guide you in developing new relationships.

Chapter 4 – Recognize Networking Opportunities

You cannot build networks unless you are able to recognize networking opportunities around you. It is imperative that you take advantage of the formal networking, informal networking, and workday opportunities that you encounter. Additionally, it is not possible to predict every network opportunity. You should always be prepared to network.

Formal Networking

Formal networking opportunities will vary with each organization. This type of networking takes place at organized social events. This ranges from professional and social groups that your peers are part of, to meetings and social functions. When you engage in formal networking, you need to appear polished and professional. It is essential that you do your homework before attending a formal networking event. For example, you should learn about the type of activities that a young professionals group at your organization participates in before going to a meeting.

Informal Networking

Informal networking happens much more frequently than formal networking. These opportunities occur every day, so you need to be aware of them. Informal opportunities occur with email interactions, coffee breaks, lunches, and group discussions. Since informal networking is not scheduled, it requires you to take initiative. For example, invite someone to join your group for lunch. Informal networking is a low-pressure way to extend your network and improving your relationships.

Workday Opportunities

You need to recognize that there are numerous networking opportunities within the workplace. Some of these may be available in programs at your organization. For example, you can greet new employees or join a mentoring group. You can also make your own workday opportunities. Bring coffee for your coworkers or keep snacks in your workspace. Remember to take the initiative when the company does not provide you with the opportunities that you would like to see.

Always Be Ready to Network

You never know when a networking opportunity will occur, so you must always be prepared. There are a few steps you can take to improve your readiness and increase your network:

- Pay attention to the people around you – Pay attention to potential opportunities.

- Look the part at all times – Keep your professional appearance.

- Make personal gestures – This helps endear you to others.

- Pay attention to changes in the industry – Maintain you expertise.

Chapter 5 – Common Networking Mistakes

Before going any further, it is time to point out the common networking mistakes that people make so that you can avoid them. We have already addressed meeting people and following through, but these remain common mistakes. Creating expectations that are too high and failing to remain professional are also common mistakes that should be avoided.

Not Meeting New People

As we have already discussed, it is not possible to expand a network without meeting new people. It is easy to consciously accept this fact while failing to act upon it. There are many reasons why people fail to follow this basic rule. Some people struggle with this because of their personalities. Others have a list of excuses that they use: there is no time; they don't know where to go, etc. In reality, people will prioritize what they find important. If they believe that networking and meeting people is important, they will make an effort to do it.

Not Following Through

Following through is just as important as meeting people. Sometimes it is easy to get caught up in the meeting new contacts at the expense of following through, and may people believe that mass communication is effective enough to establish networks. It is essential, however, to follow up with each contact individually. There is a very brief window of opportunity to follow through with contacts. If you do not follow up with new contacts quickly, the contact will forget about you or conclude that you are not interested in pursuing a relationship.

High Expectations

Another common mistake is placing high expectations on networking. While it is important to place reasonable expectations on the networking, you should not make the expectations too high. There will be a learning curve as you network, and placing unreasonably high expectations on your efforts can lead to avoidance. If you feel like your efforts at networking are not fruitful, you will not attempt to improve your networking skills. Networking typically takes a great deal of time and effort before you actually see results. Be patient, and examine and adjust your techniques before giving up on networking altogether.

Being Professional

Professionalism needs to be balanced in networking. On the one hand, people confuse being professional with being distant and cold. This will not encourage people to join your social network. Networking requires a warm and friendly tone to attract others to you. On the other hand, being too familiar will make people feel uncomfortable. Take the time to get to know new contacts. Do not take liberties. It is important to maintain a level of decorum in your professional networks.

Chapter 6 – Develop Interpersonal Relationships

As we have already discussed, networking is actually relationship building. Developing and maintaining intrapersonal relationships takes the time and effort, but they are worth the payoff. Interpersonal relationships require being genuine, participating in dialogue, maintaining boundaries, and investing time. By following the information outlined in this module, you will find it easier to develop interpersonal relationships.

Be Genuine

When developing relationships, it is essential that you be genuine. Many people are prejudiced against networking because they feel that it requires being fake and manipulative. In reality, however, interpersonal relationships require people to be genuine. Build relationships on common interests and passions. It is better to stop your efforts to connect with someone than build a relationship on false pretense. Identify your interests and passions, and be prepared to discuss them with others. This will not only show that you are genuine but also give insight into your strengths and skills.

Dialogue

We have already addressed the importance of listening and communication. Developing strong interpersonal relationships requires successful dialogue. This demands an understanding of all that dialogue entails. Dialogue is a two-way method of communication that promotes understanding. It incorporates active listening and polite conversation.

Steps to Dialogue:

- Listen actively and without interrupting.

- Be respectful even when you disagree.

- Resist the urge to argue when you respond.

Maintain Boundaries

All relationships require boundaries, and networking relationships are no exception. It is essential that you establish your own boundaries and respect the boundaries that other people have. If you do not establish boundaries, you will find yourself the stressed and overworked. You must create personal boundaries that fit your individual needs. There are steps anyone can take to help establish and keep personal boundaries.

- Establish time in your schedule for yourself and protect it.

- Communicate your boundaries.

- Learn to say no, and explain why.

- Prepare an appropriate response for people who violate your boundaries.

Invest Time

Like any other relationship, the relationships in your network require you to invest time. Given the busy schedule that most people have, it is easy to overlook networking contacts, particularly at work. It is not enough to simply run into people at work, you need to set aside time to reach out to your individual contacts. This typically requires carving time out in your schedule. Take time to make calls, send emails, and meet with your contacts. You do not have to carve out large chunks of time. Simply make the effort to invest in your contacts.

Chapter 7 – Online Networking Tools

Taking part in the networking requires using the appropriate tools. Fortunately, the internet provides a number of online networking tools that will assist your networking activities. Commonly used networking tools include popular social networks, blogs, chat rooms, and email. Implementing these tools will allow you to easily keep up with your contacts.

Social Networks

There are numerous social media networks. Three networks that are commonly used in business are Facebook, LinkedIn, and Twitter.

Facebook

Originally created for college students, Facebook has become a tool commonly used by business professionals. The site uploads comments, images, and video. You connect to people on Facebook by friending them, which gives you access to their page.

Twitter

Twitter is called a microblog. Tweets or statements uploaded are limited to 140 characters each. You connect to people by following them, and hashtags are used to label the content of tweets and create trends.

LinkedIn

LinkedIn is unique because it is a professional social network. Users create profiles with their areas of expertise and work history, similar to a resume. Linking with professional connections allows you to endorse them and them to endorse you.

You must be careful about what you post on social media. With each social network, you run the risk of over sharing. If you have any doubt that something is inappropriate, do not post it.

Blogs

Blogs are useful tools that showcase your expertise in different areas. They can also be used for networking.

Tips to Network with Blogs:

- Limit post to topics that you understand well.

- Link posts to social media and other sites.

- Comment on blogs written by other people to begin a dialogue.

- Share blog posts from other people.

- Interview contacts for blog posts.

Chat Rooms

Chat rooms are a bit more difficult to navigate than social networks are. They are online networks where people talk about specific topics. Chat rooms, however, are helpful for meeting new people who are interested in similar subjects. There are numerous chat rooms with a variety of topics. You simply choose one that you are interested in and find a conversation thread that looks promising. You can ask your coworkers if they frequent any chat rooms. People behave better in some chat rooms than others. If you find a chat room is not conducive to dialogue, leave it and find one that is more suitable.

Email

Most people are familiar with email. Email can be used for work or personal use, and it is the most commonly used networking tool. It allows you to maintain contact with people in your network without being intrusive. There are a few tips that will help you email coworkers effectively when attempting to network:

- Have a point, and place it in the subject line.

- Individualize emails, and avoid mass emails when possible.

- Be brief (keep emails close to 150 words).

- Make offers (do not simply send requests).

Emails are easy to use; so do not make them your only method of communication. It is important that you connect with people in different ways.

Chapter 8 - Time Management

Making networking a priority requires time management skills. When it comes to time management in networking, it is important to prioritize contacts and schedule activities. Connecting online and organizing activities for groups will also help you manage your time while developing relationships within your network.

Prioritize Contacts

Some contacts are more useful or more interested in developing relationships than others. When managing your time, you need to prioritize your contacts. Begin by creating a list of your contacts. Next, prioritize them according to the following information:

1. Is interested in connecting with you

2. Has useful connections

3. Has useful knowledge

Begin with your high priority contacts, and work your way down the list when connecting with people. It is more important to reach your high priority contacts first since they are more likely to be active parts of your network.

Create Group Activities

A good way to manage your network is by organizing group activities. Schedule some time each week to meet with your contacts outside the office. This is a great opportunity to expand your network and keep in touch with your contacts. These activities should be casual meeting times to get to know people outside of the workplace. Group activities do not have to be grand affairs. Consider fun activities that many people in your group will enjoy such as games, dining, bowling, movies, etc.

Connect Online

Connecting online is essential to networking. We have already discussed the different online tools. It is essential, however, that you use these tools regularly. It is not enough to simply join social networks and start a blog. You need to update regularly to keep your connections interested, and you need to comment and dialogue on other social networking sites and blogs.

Schedule time to connect online each day. You do not have to use each online tool daily. Divide your time between the tools that are most important and will reach the maximum number of people. For example, you may want to blog once a week, email daily, and update social media three to five times a week.

Schedule Your Networking Activities

Networking activities need to be scheduled or you will forget about them. A good rule of thumb is to schedule out a week in advance and make adjustments at the end of each day. Your schedule needs to include time for online networks, group activities, and private meetings. Remember that the weekly schedule is not set in stone, but creating it makes networking a priority so that you are less likely to neglect your networking activities.

Maintaining Relationships Over Time

Once you have built your network, it is essential that you maintain these relationships for the long term. It is easy to forget about established relationships as you pursue new ones to grow your network. Ignoring established connections, however, can cause individuals to feel betrayed and unwanted. This will not help your reputation with their social circle in the office.

Contact Networks Regularly

Contacting networks regularly may seem like a no brainer, but it is a rule that is all too often ignored. It is not enough to contact people with group messages or invite them to group activities. You need to reach out to individuals regularly. Send personal emails, talk on the phone, meet for coffee, or enjoy an activity together. It is not essential to connect this way on a daily or even weekly basis. Going for months without any personal contact, however, will send the message that you do not value the relationship you have already developed.

Be Honest

Any functional relationship requires honesty. This is particularly true in the workplace where people tend to be more competitive. Never lie or misrepresent yourself to your contacts. The internet makes it much easier for lies to be discovered, and you relationship will be irreparably harmed. Practicing honesty, however, does not require over sharing. You need to reveal what affects your coworkers such as new data, news, and ways you can assist them. You are not obligated to share your personal life in any detail.

Never over promise or make sweeping statements. No one likes to admit not knowing something, but providing false information is much worse. If you are not sure about something, tell your contacts that you will discover the facts and get back to them. This will give you a reputation as a good source of information.

Give Personal Attention

Contacting people in your network is important, but it is equally important to provide them all with personal attention. This is where active listening comes in handy. By paying attention to what your contacts say, you will understand their needs and interests. Rather than sending a standard form email, you will be able to send information that you know will the receiver will appreciate. You will also be able to offer the assistance when your contact needs.

Always respond as soon as possible when you are contacted. Even if you need to look something up first, respond and say that you will have an answer soon. This lets the contacts know that you see them as priorities instead of afterthoughts. Going a step further to provide personal attention will serve to improve your networking relationships.

Limit Networks to a Manageable Size

The definition of a manageable size will vary with each individually. For example, someone who has no family ties may have more time to socialize than someone who does not. Outside clubs, hobbies, etc. will also affect the time that you have to devote to managing your networks. Not keeping your network to a manageable size will result in networking failure. You will not be able to give any of your network personalized attention. There are a few factors you need to consider when reviewing your network:

- Is everyone in the network committed to growing the relationship? – If the answer is no, you need to develop the relationships further or remove them from your network.

- Do you personally know everyone in the network? – Again, remove people you do not know unless you feel that there is hope for developing the relationship.

You should review your contacts periodically to keep your network to a manageable size. Additionally, you need to be particular about who you choose to network with in the first place. If you do not see a future for a relationship, do not waste time pursuing it.

Additional Titles

The 90 Minute Guide series of books covers a variety of general business skills and are intended to be completed in 90 minutes or less. It is an effective way for building your skill set and can be used to acquire professional development units needed by project managers and other industries to maintain their certification. For the availability of titles please see

https://www.silvercitypublications.com/shop/.

No. 1 - Appreciative Inquiry

No. 2 - Assertiveness and Self Control

No. 3 - Attention Management

No. 4 - Body Language Basics

No. 5 - Business Acumen

No. 6 - Business and Etiquette

No. 7 - Change Management

No. 8 - Coaching and Mentoring

No. 9 - Communications Strategies

No. 10 - Conflict Resolution

No. 11 - Creative Problem Solving

No. 12 - Delivering Constructive Criticism

No. 13 - Developing Creativity

No. 14 - Developing Emotional Intelligence

No. 15 - Developing Interpersonal Skills

No. 16 - Developing Social Intelligence

No. 17 - Employee Motivation

No. 18 - Facilitation Skills

No. 19 - Goal Setting and Getting Things Done

No. 20 - Knowledge Management Fundamentals

No. 21 - Leadership and Influence

No. 22 - Lean Process and Six Sigma Basics

No. 23 - Managing Anger

No. 24 - Meeting Management

No. 25 - Negotiation Skills

No. 26 - Networking Inside a Company

No. 27 - Networking Outside a Company

No. 28 - Office Politics for Managers

No. 29 - Organizational Skills

No. 30 - Performance Management

No. 31 - Presentation Skills

No. 32 - Public Speaking

No. 33 - Servant Leadership

No. 34 - Team Building for Management

No. 35 - Team Work and Team Building

No. 36 - Time Management

No. 37 - Top 10 Soft Skills You Need

No. 38 - Virtual Team Building and Management